T0163627

Grammaropolis PRESENTS

Wonderful Words
For Eighth Grade

VOCABULARY AND WRITING WORKBOOK

BY ORDER OF

The Mayor of Grammaropolis

Grammaropolis LLC hereby gives teachers permission to photocopy pages from this book for classroom use only. Reproduction for any other use is not permitted, in whole or in part, for storage in a retrieval system or transmission in any form or by any means, electronic, mechanical, photocopying, recording, or otherwise, without written permission from the Publisher. For information regarding permission, write to Grammaropolis LLC, c/o Six Foot Press, 4200 Montrose Blvd., Houston, TX 77006.

Written by Christopher Knight
Interior Design by Christopher Knight
Cover Design by Mckee Frazior
Grammaropolis Character Design by Powerhouse Animation & Mckee Frazior

ISBN: 9781644420584
Copyright © 2021 by Grammaropolis LLC
All rights reserved.
Published by Six Foot Press
Printed in the U.S.A.

Grammaropolis.com
SixFootPress.com

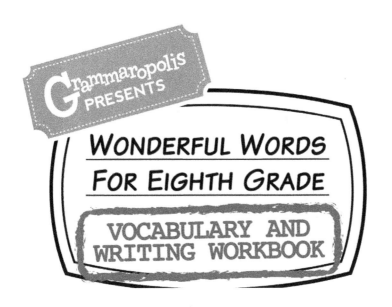

Grammaropolis
PRESENTS

WONDERFUL WORDS
FOR EIGHTH GRADE

VOCABULARY AND
WRITING WORKBOOK

GRAMMAROPOLIS BOOKS

HOUSTON

FROM THE DESK OF THE MAYOR

Greetings, fellow wordsmith!

Thank you so much for using this workbook. I hope you have fun learning some new vocabulary words!

As you know, many words can act as multiple parts of speech; it all depends on how they're used in the sentence. For the sake of clarity and simplicity (and because we didn't have enough space on the page!), the definitions in this workbook include only one part of speech for each word.

It's great to know a lot of vocabulary words, but the real reason we expand our vocabulary is so that we can communicate more effectively. That's why I've added a writing exercise, with optional prompts, at the end of each section.

Thanks again for visiting Grammaropolis. I hope you enjoy your stay!

—The Mayor

TABLE OF CONTENTS

HOW TO USE THE VOCABULARY PAGES

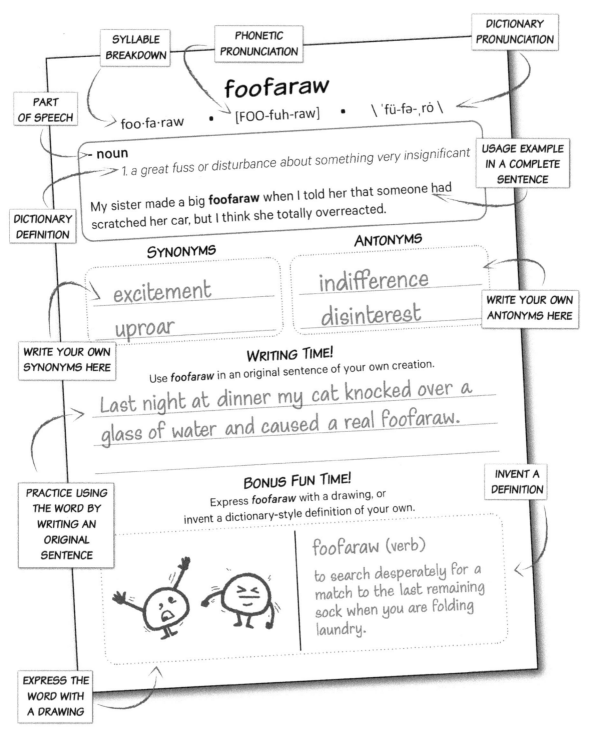

SYLLABLE BREAKDOWN

PHONETIC PRONUNCIATION

DICTIONARY PRONUNCIATION

foofaraw

PART OF SPEECH

foo·fa·raw • [FOO-fuh-raw] • \ ˈfü-fə-ˌrȯ \

noun

USAGE EXAMPLE IN A COMPLETE SENTENCE

1. a great fuss or disturbance about something very insignificant

My sister made a big **foofaraw** when I told her that someone had scratched her car, but I think she totally overreacted.

DICTIONARY DEFINITION

SYNONYMS

ANTONYMS

excitement

uproar

indifference

disinterest

WRITE YOUR OWN ANTONYMS HERE

WRITE YOUR OWN SYNONYMS HERE

WRITING TIME!
Use *foofaraw* in an original sentence of your own creation.

Last night at dinner my cat knocked over a glass of water and caused a real foofaraw.

PRACTICE USING THE WORD BY WRITING AN ORIGINAL SENTENCE

BONUS FUN TIME!
Express *foofaraw* with a drawing, or invent a dictionary-style definition of your own.

INVENT A DEFINITION

foofaraw (verb)

to search desperately for a match to the last remaining sock when you are folding laundry.

EXPRESS THE WORD WITH A DRAWING

Important Note: Synonyms and antonyms for nouns might be harder to come up with than they are for verbs and adjectives, but do your best!

THE PARTS OF SPEECH REVIEW

Every word acts as at least one of the eight parts of speech. In this workbook, you'll find nouns, verbs, and adjectives. Here are some things you need to remember about them!

NOUNS

A noun can name a person, place, thing, or idea.

Naming a person:
Jason is my very best **friend**.

Naming a place:
Becks Prime is my favorite **restaurant**.

Naming a thing:
That **ball** is my favorite **toy**.

Naming an idea:
Honesty and **loyalty** are my best **qualities**.

VERBS

An action verb expresses mental or physical action, and a linking verb expresses a state of being.

Expressing physical action:
Richard **jumped** across the river.

Expressing mental action:
Richard **considered** jumping across the river.

Expressing a state of being:
Richard **feels** bad. He **is** sorry for jumping across the river.

ADJECTIVES

*An adjective modifies a noun or a pronoun and tells **what kind, which one, how much**, or **how many**.*

Modifying a noun:
The **quick brown** fox jumped over the **enormous red** fence at the **first** sign of trouble.

Modifying a pronoun:
They are **satisfied** with the answer, but I am still **curious**.

There are five other parts of speech you won't find in this workbook, but that doesn't mean they're not important!

ADVERBS

*An adverb modifies a verb, an adjective, or another adverb and tells **how, where, when**, or **to what extent**.*

PRONOUNS

A pronoun takes the place of one or more nouns or pronouns.

PREPOSITIONS

A preposition shows a logical relationship or locates an object in time or space.

CONJUNCTIONS

A conjunction joins words or word groups.

INTERJECTIONS

An interjection expresses strong or mild emotion.

SECTION ONE: WORD PREVIEW
Welcome to your ten new favorite words!

When you encounter a new word, take a moment to consider what it might mean.

1. Think about the word and circle what part of speech you think it is. *(Many words can act as more than one part of speech, depending on how they're used in the sentence, so only choose one part of speech below.)*

2. Come up with a brief definition of the word in the part of speech you've chosen. It doesn't have to be the *correct* definition—just do your best.

conclude
Part of Speech: noun   verb   adjective

*Definition:*_____

_____

spontaneous
Part of Speech: noun   verb   adjective

*Definition:*_____

_____

ambiguous
Part of Speech: noun   verb   adjective

*Definition:*_____

_____

pseudonym
Part of Speech: noun   verb   adjective

*Definition:*_____

_____

novice
Part of Speech: noun   verb   adjective

*Definition:*_____

_____

imminent
Part of Speech: noun   verb   adjective

*Definition:*_____

_____

variable
Part of Speech: noun   verb   adjective

*Definition:*_____

_____

elapse
Part of Speech: noun   verb   adjective

*Definition:*_____

_____

reverberate
Part of Speech: noun   verb   adjective

*Definition:*_____

_____

consistent
Part of Speech: noun   verb   adjective

*Definition:*_____

_____

conclude

con·clude • [kuhn-klOOd] • \ kənˈklo͞od \

> **- verb**
>
> 1. *to bring (something) to an end;*
> 2. *to arrive at a judgment or opinion by reasoning*
>
> I **concluded** my speech by telling a dumb joke and wishing everyone in the audience a good night.

SYNONYMS

ANTONYMS

WRITING TIME!
Use *conclude* in an original sentence of your own creation.

BONUS FUN TIME!
Express *conclude* with a drawing, or
invent a dictionary-style definition of your own.

spontaneous

spon·ta·ne·ous • [spahn-tAY-nee-uhs] • \ spänˈtānēəs \

> **- adjective**
>   *1. (of an event) occurring without apparent external cause;*
>   *2. (of a person) having an open, natural, and uninhibited manner*
>
> Julie didn't plan for anyone to spend the night, but a **spontaneous** slumber party happened anyway.

SYNONYMS

ANTONYMS

WRITING TIME!
Use *spontaneous* in an original sentence of your own creation.

BONUS FUN TIME!
Express *spontaneous* with a drawing, or
invent a dictionary-style definition of your own.

ambiguous

am·big·u·ous • [am-bI-gyuh-wuhs] • \ amˈbigyo͞oəs \

- adjective

1. open to more than one interpretation;

2. unclear or inexact because a choice has not been made

I think you made your answer **ambiguous** so that we wouldn't be sure what you'd actually decided.

SYNONYMS

ANTONYMS

WRITING TIME!

Use *ambiguous* in an original sentence of your own creation.

BONUS FUN TIME!

Express *ambiguous* with a drawing, or
invent a dictionary-style definition of your own.

pseudonym

pseu·do·nym • [sOO-duh-nim] • \ ˈso͞odənim \

> **- noun**
>
> *1. a fictitious name, especially one used by an author*
>
> Stephen King used to publish some of his books under the **pseudonym** of Richard Bachman.

SYNONYMS

ANTONYMS

WRITING TIME!
Use *pseudonym* in an original sentence of your own creation.

BONUS FUN TIME!
Express *pseudonym* with a drawing, or
invent a dictionary-style definition of your own.

novice

nov·ice   •   [nAHv-uhs]   •   \ ˈnävəs \

- noun

1. a person new to or inexperienced in a field or situation

I'm a **novice** when it comes to car maintenance, but my sister is an experienced mechanic.

SYNONYMS

ANTONYMS

WRITING TIME!
Use *novice* in an original sentence of your own creation.

BONUS FUN TIME!
Express *novice* with a drawing, or
invent a dictionary-style definition of your own.

imminent

im·mi·nent   •   [Im-uh-nuhnt]   •   \ ˈimənənt \

- **adjective**

1. about to happen

We had to run through the airport because our departure was **imminent**, and we were nowhere near the right gate.

SYNONYMS

ANTONYMS

WRITING TIME!
Use *imminent* in an original sentence of your own creation.

BONUS FUN TIME!
Express *imminent* with a drawing, or
invent a dictionary-style definition of your own.

variable

var·i·a·ble • [vAIR-ee-uh-buhl] • \ ˈverēəb(ə)l \

- adjective

1. not consistent or having a fixed pattern;

2. able to be changed or adapted

The restaurant's menu is **variable**, so I never know for sure what's going to be on it.

SYNONYMS

ANTONYMS

WRITING TIME!

Use *variable* in an original sentence of your own creation.

BONUS FUN TIME!

Express *variable* with a drawing, or
invent a dictionary-style definition of your own.

elapse

e·lapse   •   [i-lAps]   •   \ əˈlaps \

- verb

1. (of time) to pass or go by

How many minutes have **elapsed** since we put the cookies in the oven?

SYNONYMS

ANTONYMS

WRITING TIME!

Use *elapse* in an original sentence of your own creation.

BONUS FUN TIME!

Express *elapse* with a drawing, or
invent a dictionary-style definition of your own.

reverberate

re·ver·ber·ate • [ri-vUHR-buhr-rayt] • \ rəˈvərbəˌrāt \

- verb

1. *(of a loud noise) to be repeated several times as an echo;*
2. *to have continuing and serious effects*

Tasha dropped the big metal bowl, and the ensuing sound **reverberated** through the empty warehouse.

SYNONYMS

_____

_____

_____

ANTONYMS

_____

_____

_____

WRITING TIME!

Use *reverberate* in an original sentence of your own creation.

_____

_____

BONUS FUN TIME!

Express *reverberate* with a drawing, or
invent a dictionary-style definition of your own.

consistent

con·sist·ent   •   [kuhn-sIs-tuhnt]   •   \ kənˈsistənt \

- adjective

1. acting or done in the same way over time, especially so as to be fair or accurate

In order to build a new habit, it helps to be **consistent** with your effort; otherwise, it's difficult for the new behavior to take hold.

SYNONYMS

ANTONYMS

WRITING TIME!

Use *consistent* in an original sentence of your own creation.

BONUS FUN TIME!

Express *consistent* with a drawing, or
invent a dictionary-style definition of your own.

SECTION ONE: WORD REVIEW

Congratulations on learning ten amazing new words! Remember that the whole point of learning new vocabulary is actually to use it, so let's put your new vocabulary to use.

1. Review the words you've learned. Consider what ideas come to mind when you say the words. How about when you read the definitions?
2. Circle at least **two** of your favorites. You'll get to use these when you write your very own story!

conclude — verb
1. to bring (something) to an end;
2. to arrive at a judgment or opinion by reasoning

spontaneous — adjective
1. (of an event) occurring without apparent external cause;
2. (of a person) having an open, natural, and uninhibited manner

ambiguous — adjective
1. open to more than one interpretation;
2. unclear or inexact because a choice has not been made

pseudonym — noun
1. a fictitious name, especially one used by an author

novice — noun
1. a person new to or inexperienced in a field or situation

imminent — adjective
1. about to happen

variable — adjective
1. not consistent or having a fixed pattern;
2. able to be changed or adapted

elapse — verb
1. (of time) to pass or go by

reverberate — verb
1. (of a loud noise) to be repeated several times as an echo;
2. to have continuing and serious effects

consistent — adjective
1. acting or done in the same way over time, especially so as to be fair or accurate

STORY ONE

1. List the words you've chosen:

_____

2. Write a story that incorporates all of your chosen words. If you can't think of anything to write about, consider these suggestions:
   - **Write a story that ends with the main character having to make an extremely difficult decision.**
   - **Write a story that takes place in an ice cream factory.**

Title: _____

_____

_____

_____

_____

_____

_____

_____

_____

_____

Wonderful Words for Eighth Grade Vocabulary & Writing Workbook ©2021 Grammaropolis LLC

Wonderful Words for Eighth Grade Vocabulary & Writing Workbook ©2021 Grammaropolis LLC

SECTION TWO: WORD PREVIEW
Welcome to your ten new favorite words!

When you encounter a new word, take a moment to consider what it might mean.

1. Think about the word and circle what part of speech you think it is. *(Many words can act as more than one part of speech, depending on how they're used in the sentence, **so only choose one part of speech below.**)*

2. Come up with a brief definition of the word in the part of speech you've chosen. It doesn't have to be the *correct* definition—just do your best.

despondent
Part of Speech: noun   verb   adjective

Definition:_____

_____

endeavor
Part of Speech: noun   verb   adjective

Definition:_____

_____

depict
Part of Speech: noun   verb   adjective

Definition:_____

_____

obsolete
Part of Speech: noun   verb   adjective

Definition:_____

_____

plagiarize
Part of Speech: noun   verb   adjective

Definition:_____

_____

gruesome
Part of Speech: noun   verb   adjective

Definition:_____

_____

profound
Part of Speech: noun   verb   adjective

Definition:_____

_____

perish
Part of Speech: noun   verb   adjective

Definition:_____

_____

anthology
Part of Speech: noun   verb   adjective

Definition:_____

_____

merge
Part of Speech: noun   verb   adjective

Definition:_____

_____

despondent

de·spond·ent • [di-spAHn-duhnt] • \ dəˈspändənt \

- adjective

1. in low spirits from loss of hope or courage

Some of Guy's teammates were **despondent** after the other team scored a goal, but Guy implored them not to give up hope.

SYNONYMS

ANTONYMS

WRITING TIME!

Use *despondent* in an original sentence of your own creation.

BONUS FUN TIME!

Express *despondent* with a drawing, or
invent a dictionary-style definition of your own.

endeavor

en·deav·or   •   [in-dEv-uhr]   •   \ ənˈdevər \

- noun
   1. *an attempt to achieve a goal;*
   2. *an enterprise or undertaking*

Isis tried to convince the town council that building a new baseball field was a worthwhile **endeavor**.

SYNONYMS

ANTONYMS

WRITING TIME!
Use *endeavor* in an original sentence of your own creation.

BONUS FUN TIME!
Express *endeavor* with a drawing, or
invent a dictionary-style definition of your own.

depict

de·pict   •   [di-pIkt]   •   \ dəˈpikt \

- verb

1. to show or represent by a drawing, painting, or other art form

Some artists **depict** their subjects with oil paints while others prefer to use watercolor.

SYNONYMS

ANTONYMS

WRITING TIME!
Use *depict* in an original sentence of your own creation.

BONUS FUN TIME!
Express *depict* with a drawing, or
invent a dictionary-style definition of your own.

obsolete

ob·so·lete • [ahb-suh-lEEt] • \ ˌäbsəˈlēt \

- adjective

1. no longer produced or used : out of date

Electronics these days become useless and **obsolete** way too quickly.

SYNONYMS

ANTONYMS

WRITING TIME!
Use *obsolete* in an original sentence of your own creation.

BONUS FUN TIME!
Express *obsolete* with a drawing, or
invent a dictionary-style definition of your own.

plagiarize

pla·gia·rize • [plAY-juhr-riez] • \ ˈplājəˌrīz \

- verb

  1. to take the work or an idea of someone else and pass it off as one's own

Don't **plagiarize** someone else's speech; you need to write your own.

SYNONYMS

ANTONYMS

WRITING TIME!
Use *plagiarize* in an original sentence of your own creation.

BONUS FUN TIME!
Express *plagiarize* with a drawing, or
invent a dictionary-style definition of your own.

gruesome

grue·some • [grOO-suhm] • \ ˈgro͞osəm \

- adjective

1. causing repulsion or horror : grisly

I don't like watching scary movies because the violence is way too **gruesome** for me.

SYNONYMS

ANTONYMS

WRITING TIME!
Use *gruesome* in an original sentence of your own creation.

BONUS FUN TIME!
Express *gruesome* with a drawing, or
invent a dictionary-style definition of your own.

profound

pro·found   •   [pruh-fOUnd]   •   \ prəˈfound \

- adjective

1. (of a state, quality, or emotion) very great or intense;

2. (of a subject) demanding deep study or thought

We all felt a **profound** relief when we saw Yolanda making her way safely off the damaged ship.

SYNONYMS

_____

_____

_____

ANTONYMS

_____

_____

_____

WRITING TIME!

Use *profound* in an original sentence of your own creation.

_____

_____

_____

BONUS FUN TIME!

Express *profound* with a drawing, or
invent a dictionary-style definition of your own.

perish

per·ish   •   [pAIR-ish]   •   \ ˈperiSH \

- verb

1. to suffer death, typically in a violent, sudden, or untimely way

Molly was distraught when her pet parakeet unexpectedly **perished** after eating bad seeds.

SYNONYMS

ANTONYMS

WRITING TIME!

Use *perish* in an original sentence of your own creation.

BONUS FUN TIME!

Express *perish* with a drawing, or
invent a dictionary-style definition of your own.

anthology

an·thol·o·gy • [an-thAHl-uh-jee] • \ anˈTHäləjē \

- **noun**

   1. a published collection of poems or other pieces of writing;

   2. a collection of songs or musical compositions on one album

Donna collected all of the letters her mother had ever written to her and published them in an **anthology** for her children to read.

SYNONYMS

ANTONYMS

WRITING TIME!
Use *anthology* in an original sentence of your own creation.

BONUS FUN TIME!
Express *anthology* with a drawing, or
invent a dictionary-style definition of your own.

merge

merge   •   [mUHRj]   •   \ mərj \

- verb

1. to combine or cause to combine to form a single entity

If we **merge** our two bank accounts, we will probably have enough money to buy that ice cream shop!

SYNONYMS

ANTONYMS

WRITING TIME!

Use *merge* in an original sentence of your own creation.

BONUS FUN TIME!

Express *merge* with a drawing, or
invent a dictionary-style definition of your own.

SECTION TWO: WORD REVIEW

Congratulations on learning ten amazing new words! Remember that the whole point of learning new vocabulary is actually to use it, so let's put your new vocabulary to use.

1. Review the words you've learned. Consider what ideas come to mind when you say the words. How about when you read the definitions?
2. Circle at least **two** of your favorites. You'll get to use these when you write your very own story!

despondent — adjective
1. *in low spirits from loss of hope or courage*

endeavor — noun
1. *an attempt to achieve a goal;*
2. *an enterprise or undertaking*

depict — verb
1. *to show or represent by a drawing, painting, or other art form*

obsolete — adjective
1. *no longer produced or used : out of date*

plagiarize — verb
1. *to take the work or an idea of someone else and pass it off as one's own*

gruesome — adjective
1. *causing repulsion or horror : grisly*

profound — adjective
1. *(of a state, quality, or emotion) very great or intense;*
2. *(of a subject) demanding deep study or thought*

perish — verb
1. *to suffer death, typically in a violent, sudden, or untimely way*

anthology — noun
1. *a published collection of poems or other pieces of writing;*
2. *a collection of songs or musical compositions on one album*

merge — verb
1. *to combine or cause to combine to form a single entity*

STORY TWO

1. List the words you've chosen:

_____

2. Write a story that incorporates all of your chosen words. If you can't think of anything to write about, consider these suggestions:
   - **Write a story that takes place in Ancient Greece.**
   - **Write a story that starts with you losing the thing that is most important to you.**

Title: _____

_____

_____

_____

_____

_____

_____

_____

_____

_____

Wonderful Words for Eighth Grade Vocabulary & Writing Workbook ©2021 Grammaropolis LLC

SECTION THREE: WORD PREVIEW
Welcome to your ten new favorite words!

When you encounter a new word, take a moment to consider what it might mean.

    1. Think about the word and circle what part of speech you think it is. *(Many words can act as more than one part of speech, depending on how they're used in the sentence, **so only choose one part of speech below**.)*

    2. Come up with a brief definition of the word in the part of speech you've chosen. It doesn't have to be the *correct* definition—just do your best.

compel
Part of Speech: noun   verb   adjective

Definition:_____

_____

resilient
Part of Speech: noun   verb   adjective

Definition:_____

_____

conscientious
Part of Speech: noun   verb   adjective

Definition:_____

_____

conjecture
Part of Speech: noun   verb   adjective

Definition:_____

_____

anarchy
Part of Speech: noun   verb   adjective

Definition:_____

_____

amiss
Part of Speech: noun   verb   adjective

Definition:_____

_____

alternative
Part of Speech: noun   verb   adjective

Definition:_____

_____

evidence
Part of Speech: noun   verb   adjective

Definition:_____

_____

apprehend
Part of Speech: noun   verb   adjective

Definition:_____

_____

simulate
Part of Speech: noun   verb   adjective

Definition:_____

_____

compel

com·pel   •   [kuhm-pEl]   •   \ kəmˈpel \

- verb

1. to force or oblige (someone) to do something

My love of Milk Duds **compels** me to order them every time I go to the movies.

SYNONYMS

_____

_____

ANTONYMS

_____

_____

WRITING TIME!

Use *compel* in an original sentence of your own creation.

_____

_____

BONUS FUN TIME!

Express *compel* with a drawing, or
invent a dictionary-style definition of your own.

resilient

re·sil·ient   •   [ri-zIl-yuhnt]   •   \ rəˈzilyənt \

- adjective

1. able to withstand or recover quickly from difficult conditions

We all thought that the small tree would get blown away by the wind, but after the storm passed, that **resilient** little thing was still there!

SYNONYMS

_____
_____
_____

ANTONYMS

_____
_____
_____

WRITING TIME!

Use *resilient* in an original sentence of your own creation.

_____

_____

_____

BONUS FUN TIME!

Express *resilient* with a drawing, or
invent a dictionary-style definition of your own.

conscientious

con·sci·en·tious • [kahn-shee-En-chuhs] • \ ˌkän(t)SHēˈen(t)SHəs \

- adjective

1. (of a person) wishing to do what is right, especially to do one's work or duty well and thoroughly

Some people don't really care about the work they do, but most of my friends are **conscientious** when it comes to group projects.

SYNONYMS

ANTONYMS

WRITING TIME!

Use *conscientious* in an original sentence of your own creation.

BONUS FUN TIME!

Express *conscientious* with a drawing, or invent a dictionary-style definition of your own.

conjecture

con·jec·ture • [kuhn-jEk-chuhr] • \ kənˈjekCHər \

- noun

1. an opinion or conclusion formed on the basis of incomplete information

Until we have all the facts, any conclusions we come to are just **conjecture**.

SYNONYMS

_____

_____

ANTONYMS

_____

_____

WRITING TIME!

Use *conjecture* in an original sentence of your own creation.

_____

_____

BONUS FUN TIME!

Express *conjecture* with a drawing, or
invent a dictionary-style definition of your own.

anarchy

an·ar·chy • [An-uhr-kee] • \ ˈanərkē \

- **noun**

  1. *a state of disorder due to absence or nonrecognition of authority*

  As soon as the teacher walked out of the room, the class devolved into **anarchy**, and nobody cared about the rules at all.

SYNONYMS

ANTONYMS

WRITING TIME!
Use *anarchy* in an original sentence of your own creation.

BONUS FUN TIME!
Express *anarchy* with a drawing, or
invent a dictionary-style definition of your own.

amiss

a·miss • [uh-mIs] • \ əˈmis \

> **- adjective**
>   1. *not quite right;*
>   2. *inappropriate or out of place*
>
> I knew something was **amiss** when I opened the door and saw my dog's face covered in frosting.

SYNONYMS

ANTONYMS

WRITING TIME!
Use *amiss* in an original sentence of your own creation.

BONUS FUN TIME!
Express *amiss* with a drawing, or
invent a dictionary-style definition of your own.

alternative

al·ter·na·tive • [awl-tUHR-nuh-tiv] • \ ôlˈtərnədiv \

- noun

1. *one of two or more available possibilities*

The **alternative** to getting our work done right now is to wait until the morning when we are feeling more energetic.

SYNONYMS

ANTONYMS

WRITING TIME!

Use *alternative* in an original sentence of your own creation.

BONUS FUN TIME!

Express *alternative* with a drawing, or
invent a dictionary-style definition of your own.

evidence

ev·i·dence • [Ev-uh-duhns] • \ ˈevədəns \

- **noun**

   1. the available body of facts or information;

   2. signs or indications of something

It's important to consider all the **evidence** before you come to a conclusion, even if it's inconvenient to do so.

SYNONYMS

ANTONYMS

WRITING TIME!

Use *evidence* in an original sentence of your own creation.

BONUS FUN TIME!

Express *evidence* with a drawing, or
invent a dictionary-style definition of your own.

apprehend

ap·pre·hend • [ap-ri-hEnd] • \ ˌaprəˈhend \

- verb

1. to arrest (someone) for a crime

It took a while, but the detective finally **apprehended** the man who stole her pocketwatch.

SYNONYMS

_____

_____

ANTONYMS

_____

_____

WRITING TIME!

Use *apprehend* in an original sentence of your own creation.

_____

_____

_____

BONUS FUN TIME!

Express *apprehend* with a drawing, or
invent a dictionary-style definition of your own.

simulate

sim·u·late • [sIm-yuh-layt] • \ ˈsimyə͵lāt \

- verb
>   *1. to imitate the appearance or character of;*
>   *2. to produce a model of*

We can't actually go to Mars yet, so we **simulate** the Martian conditions for our astronauts in training.

SYNONYMS

ANTONYMS

WRITING TIME!
Use *simulate* in an original sentence of your own creation.

BONUS FUN TIME!
Express *simulate* with a drawing, or
invent a dictionary-style definition of your own.

Section Three: Word Review

Congratulations on learning ten amazing new words! Remember that the whole point of learning new vocabulary is actually to use it, so let's put your new vocabulary to use.

1. Review the words you've learned. Consider what ideas come to mind when you say the words. How about when you read the definitions?
2. Circle at least **two** of your favorites. You'll get to use these when you write your very own story!

compel ———— verb

1. *to force or oblige (someone) to do something*

resilient ———— adjective

1. *able to withstand or recover quickly from difficult conditions*

conscientious – adjective

1. *(of a person) wishing to do what is right, especially to do one's work or duty well and thoroughly*

conjecture ———— noun

1. *an opinion or conclusion formed on the basis of incomplete information particular period of time or in a given sample*

anarchy ———— noun

1. *a state of disorder due to absence or nonrecognition of authority*

amiss ———— adjective

1. *not quite right;*
2. *inappropriate or out of place*

alternative ———— noun

1. *one of two or more available possibilities*

evidence ———— noun

1. *the available body of facts or information;*
2. *signs or indications of something*

apprehend ———— verb

1. *to arrest (someone) for a crime*

simulate ———— verb

1. *to imitate the appearance or character of;*
2. *to produce a model of*

STORY THREE

1. List the words you've chosen:

_____

2. Write a story that incorporates all of your chosen words. If you can't think of anything to write about, consider these suggestions:
   - Write a story in which you can time travel, but your limit is only five minutes in the past.
   - Write a story in which your main character can talk to insects.

Title: _____

_____

_____

_____

_____

_____

_____

_____

_____

_____

Wonderful Words for Eighth Grade Vocabulary & Writing Workbook ©2021 Grammaropolis LLC

SECTION FOUR: WORD PREVIEW
Welcome to your ten new favorite words!

When you encounter a new word, take a moment to consider what it might mean.

1. Think about the word and circle what part of speech you think it is.
   *(Many words can act as more than one part of speech, depending on how they're used in the sentence, **so only choose one part of speech below.**)*
2. Come up with a brief definition of the word in the part of speech you've chosen. It doesn't have to be the *correct* definition—just do your best.

commence
Part of Speech: noun   verb   adjective

Definition:_____

_____

assumption
Part of Speech: noun   verb   adjective

Definition:_____

_____

audacious
Part of Speech: noun   verb   adjective

Definition:_____

_____

derive
Part of Speech: noun   verb   adjective

Definition:_____

_____

formula
Part of Speech: noun   verb   adjective

Definition:_____

_____

bisect
Part of Speech: noun   verb   adjective

Definition:_____

_____

tirade
Part of Speech: noun   verb   adjective

Definition:_____

_____

imperative
Part of Speech: noun   verb   adjective

Definition:_____

_____

assimilate
Part of Speech: noun   verb   adjective

Definition:_____

_____

evoke
Part of Speech: noun   verb   adjective

Definition:_____

_____

commence

com·mence • [kuh-mEns] • \ kəˈmens \

- verb

1. *to begin : start*

The performance will **commence** precisely at 8:00PM.

SYNONYMS

ANTONYMS

WRITING TIME!
Use *commence* in an original sentence of your own creation.

BONUS FUN TIME!
Express *commence* with a drawing, or
invent a dictionary-style definition of your own.

assumption

as·sump·tion • [uh-sUHmpshUHn] • \ əˈsəm(p)SH(ə)n \

- noun

1. a thing that is accepted as true or as certain, without proof;

2. the action of taking on power or responsibility

I was operating under the **assumption** that my dog would not chew on my action figures, but that didn't turn out to be the case.

SYNONYMS

ANTONYMS

WRITING TIME!

Use *assumption* in an original sentence of your own creation.

BONUS FUN TIME!

Express *assumption* with a drawing, or
invent a dictionary-style definition of your own.

audacious

au·da·cious   •   [aw-dAY-shuhs]   •   \ ôˈdāSHəs \

- adjective

1. showing a willingness to take surprisingly bold risks

The protagonist and her twin sister crafted an **audacious** plan to take back their parents' stolen wedding rings.

SYNONYMS

ANTONYMS

WRITING TIME!
Use *audacious* in an original sentence of your own creation.

BONUS FUN TIME!
Express *audacious* with a drawing, or
invent a dictionary-style definition of your own.

derive

de·rive • [di-rIEv] • \ dəˈrīv \

- verb

1. to obtain something from (a specified source);

2. to arise from or originate in (a specified source)

That particular style of dance **derives** from the Pampas region of Argentina,

---

SYNONYMS

ANTONYMS

WRITING TIME!
Use *derive* in an original sentence of your own creation.

BONUS FUN TIME!
Express *derive* with a drawing, or
invent a dictionary-style definition of your own.

formula

for·mu·la • [fOR-myuh-luh] • \ ˈfôrmyələ \

- **noun**

   1. a method, statement, or procedure for achieving something;
   2. a list of ingredients for or constituents of something

   We have discovered the perfect **formula** for being happy: lots of ice cream and no homework.

SYNONYMS

ANTONYMS

WRITING TIME!
Use *formula* in an original sentence of your own creation.

BONUS FUN TIME!
Express *formula* with a drawing, or
invent a dictionary-style definition of your own.

bisect

bi·sect   •   [bIE-sekt]   •   \ bīˈsekt \

- **verb**

   1. to divide into two parts

The freeway **bisects** what used to be a single thriving neighborhood.

SYNONYMS

ANTONYMS

WRITING TIME!
Use *bisect* in an original sentence of your own creation.

BONUS FUN TIME!
Express *bisect* with a drawing, or
invent a dictionary-style definition of your own.

tirade

ti·rade   •   [tIE-rayd]   •   \ 'tī͵rād \

- noun

1. *a long, angry speech of criticism or accusation*

After the **tirade** that customer just delivered, you'd think the waiter put cockroaches in her soup.

SYNONYMS

ANTONYMS

WRITING TIME!
Use *tirade* in an original sentence of your own creation.

BONUS FUN TIME!
Express *tirade* with a drawing, or
invent a dictionary-style definition of your own.

imperative

im·per·a·tive • [im-pAIR-uh-tiv] • \ əmˈperədiv \

- adjective

1. of vital importance : crucial

It is **imperative** that we all work together to build a thriving and just society.

SYNONYMS

ANTONYMS

WRITING TIME!

Use *imperative* in an original sentence of your own creation.

BONUS FUN TIME!

Express *imperative* with a drawing, or
invent a dictionary-style definition of your own.

assimilate

as·sim·i·late • [uh-sIm-uh-layt] • \ əˈsiməˌlāt \

- verb
1. to take in (information, ideas, or culture) and understand fully;
2. to become absorbed and integrated

It took a while for the student to **assimilate** all the information in her textbook, but she finally figured everything out.

SYNONYMS

ANTONYMS

WRITING TIME!
Use *assimilate* in an original sentence of your own creation.

BONUS FUN TIME!
Express *assimilate* with a drawing, or
invent a dictionary-style definition of your own.

evoke

e·voke • [i-vOHk] • \ əˈvōk \

- verb
    1. to bring or recall to the conscious mind;
    2. to elicit (a response)

That painting **evokes** a feeling of tranquil sadness in everyone who sees it.

Synonyms

Antonyms

Writing Time!
Use *evoke* in an original sentence of your own creation.

Bonus Fun Time!
Express *evoke* with a drawing, or
invent a dictionary-style definition of your own.

SECTION FOUR: WORD REVIEW

Congratulations on learning ten amazing new words! Remember that the whole point of learning new vocabulary is actually to use it, so let's put your new vocabulary to use.

1. Review the words you've learned. Consider what ideas come to mind when you say the words. How about when you read the definitions?
2. Circle at least **two** of your favorites. You'll get to use these when you write your very own story!

commence ——— verb

1. to begin : start

assumption ——— noun

1. a thing that is accepted as true or as certain, without proof;
2. the action of taking on power or responsibility

audacious ——— adjective

1. showing a willingness to take surprisingly bold risks

derive ——— verb

1. to obtain something from (a specified source);
2. to arise from or originate in (a specified source)

formula ——— noun

1. a method, statement, or procedure for achieving something;
2. a list of ingredients for or constituents of something

bisect ——— verb

1. to divide into two parts

tirade ——— noun

1. a long, angry speech of criticism or accusation

imperative ——— adjective

1. of vital importance : crucial

assimilate ——— verb

1. to take in (information, ideas, or culture) and understand fully;
2. to become absorbed and integrated

evoke ——— verb

1. to bring or recall to the conscious mind;
2. to elicit (a response)

STORY FOUR

1. List the words you've chosen:

_____

2. Write a story that incorporates all of your chosen words. If you can't think of anything to write about, consider these suggestions:

   - Write a story in that takes place inside the world of the last dream that you can remember.

   - Write a story that starts, "If I had only known the combination. . ."

Title: _____

_____

_____

_____

_____

_____

_____

_____

_____

_____

_____

Wonderful Words for Eighth Grade Vocabulary & Writing Workbook ©2021 Grammaropolis LLC

SECTION FIVE: WORD PREVIEW
Welcome to your ten new favorite words!

When you encounter a new word, take a moment to consider what it might mean.

1. Think about the word and circle what part of speech you think it is.
   (Many words can act as more than one part of speech, depending on how they're used in the sentence, **so only choose one part of speech below.**)
2. Come up with a brief definition of the word in the part of speech you've chosen. It doesn't have to be the *correct* definition—just do your best.

procedure
Part of Speech: noun   verb   adjective

Definition:_____

_____

prevalent
Part of Speech: noun   verb   adjective

Definition:_____

_____

abhor
Part of Speech: noun   verb   adjective

Definition:_____

_____

specific
Part of Speech: noun   verb   adjective

Definition:_____

_____

proprietor
Part of Speech: noun   verb   adjective

Definition:_____

_____

apathy
Part of Speech: noun   verb   adjective

Definition:_____

_____

rebuke
Part of Speech: noun   verb   adjective

Definition:_____

_____

despicable
Part of Speech: noun   verb   adjective

Definition:_____

_____

bizarre
Part of Speech: noun   verb   adjective

Definition:_____

_____

authority
Part of Speech: noun   verb   adjective

Definition:_____

_____

procedure

pro·ce·dure • [pruh-sEE-juhr] • \ prəˈsējər \

- noun
1. an established or official way of doing something;
2. a surgical operation

When you start a new job, you have to learn the proper **procedures** at your new workplace.

SYNONYMS

_____

_____

_____

ANTONYMS

_____

_____

_____

WRITING TIME!
Use *procedure* in an original sentence of your own creation.

_____

_____

_____

BONUS FUN TIME!
Express *procedure* with a drawing, or
invent a dictionary-style definition of your own.

prevalent

prev·a·lent   •   [prEv-uh-luhnt]   •   \ ˈprev(ə)lənt \

- adjective

1. widespread in a particular area or at a particular time

Freckles are **prevalent** among people who spend a lot of time in the sun.

SYNONYMS

ANTONYMS

WRITING TIME!
Use *prevalent* in an original sentence of your own creation.

BONUS FUN TIME!
Express *prevalent* with a drawing, or
invent a dictionary-style definition of your own.

abhor

ab·hor   •   [uhb-hOR]   •   \ abˈhôr \

- verb

    1. to regard with disgust and hatred

I **abhor** people who are mean to animals.

SYNONYMS

ANTONYMS

WRITING TIME!

Use *abhor* in an original sentence of your own creation.

BONUS FUN TIME!

Express *abhor* with a drawing, or
invent a dictionary-style definition of your own.

specific

spe·cif·ic • [spi-sIf-ik] • \ spəˈsifik \

- adjective

  1. clearly defined or identified;

  2. precise and clear in making statements or issuing instructions

Is there a **specific** book you want me to read, or can I just grab anything from the shelf?

SYNONYMS

ANTONYMS

WRITING TIME!

Use *specific* in an original sentence of your own creation.

_____

_____

BONUS FUN TIME!

Express *specific* with a drawing, or
invent a dictionary-style definition of your own.

proprietor

pro·pri·e·tor   •   [pruh-prIE-uh-tuhr]   •   \ p(r)əˈprīədər \

- noun

1. the owner of a business, or a holder of property

My aunt retired, moved to the mountains, and became the **proprietor** of a small bed and breakfast.

SYNONYMS

ANTONYMS

WRITING TIME!
Use *proprietor* in an original sentence of your own creation.

BONUS FUN TIME!
Express *proprietor* with a drawing, or
invent a dictionary-style definition of your own.

apathy

ap·a·thy   •   [Ap-uh-thee]   •   \ ˈapəTHē \

- noun

1. lack of interest, enthusiasm, or concern

Many people care passionately about the environment, but some people have nothing but **apathy** about it.

SYNONYMS

ANTONYMS

WRITING TIME!
Use *apathy* in an original sentence of your own creation.

BONUS FUN TIME!
Express *apathy* with a drawing, or
invent a dictionary-style definition of your own.

rebuke

re·buke   •   [ri-byOOk]   •   \ rə'byo͞ok \

> **- verb**
>
>   *1. to express sharp disapproval or criticism of (someone) because of their behavior or actions*
>
> My dog walked away with her tail between her legs after I **rebuked** her for chewing up my favorite slippers.

SYNONYMS

_____

_____

ANTONYMS

_____

_____

WRITING TIME!

Use *rebuke* in an original sentence of your own creation.

_____

_____

BONUS FUN TIME!

Express *rebuke* with a drawing, or
invent a dictionary-style definition of your own.

despicable

des·pi·ca·ble • [di-spIk-uh-buhl] • \ dəˈspikəb(ə)l \

- **adjective**

    1. deserving of hatred and contempt

    Fred thinks it's **despicable** for people to kick their dogs, and I agree!

SYNONYMS

ANTONYMS

WRITING TIME!
Use *despicable* in an original sentence of your own creation.

BONUS FUN TIME!
Express *despicable* with a drawing, or
invent a dictionary-style definition of your own.

bizarre

bi·zarre   •   [buh-zAHR]   •   \ bəˈzär \

- adjective

1. very strange or unusual, especially so as to cause interest or amusement

Elmer delivered a really **bizarre** speech last night, and even though none of us knew what he was talking about, we all enjoyed it.

Synonyms

Antonyms

Writing Time!

Use *bizarre* in an original sentence of your own creation.

Bonus Fun Time!

Express *bizarre* with a drawing, or
invent a dictionary-style definition of your own.

authority

au·thor·i·ty • [uh-thOR-uh-tee] • \ əˈTHôrədē \

- noun
> *1. the power or right to give orders or make decisions;*
> *2. a person or organization having power or control*

Anyone who wants to play in my treehouse has to recognize my **authority** to make the rules.

SYNONYMS

ANTONYMS

WRITING TIME!
Use *authority* in an original sentence of your own creation.

BONUS FUN TIME!
Express *authority* with a drawing, or
invent a dictionary-style definition of your own.

SECTION FIVE: WORD REVIEW

Congratulations on learning ten amazing new words! Remember that the whole point of learning new vocabulary is actually to use it, so let's put your new vocabulary to use.

1. Review the words you've learned. Consider what ideas come to mind when you say the words. How about when you read the definitions?
2. Circle at least **two** of your favorites. You'll get to use these when you write your very own story!

procedure — noun
1. an established or official way of doing something;
2. a surgical operation

prevalent — adjective
1. widespread in a particular area or at a particular time

abhor — verb
1. to regard with disgust and hatred

specific — adjective
1. clearly defined or identified;
2. precise and clear in making statements or issuing instructions

proprietor — noun
1. the owner of a business, or a holder of property

apathy — noun
1. lack of interest, enthusiasm, or concern

rebuke — verb
1. to express sharp disapproval or criticism of (someone) because of their behavior or actions

despicable — adjective
1. deserving of hatred and contempt

bizarre — adjective
1. very strange or unusual, especially so as to cause interest or amusement

authority — noun
1. the power or right to give orders or make decisions;
2. a person or organization having power or control

STORY FIVE

1. List the words you've chosen:

_____

2. Write a story that incorporates all of your chosen words. If you can't think of anything to write about, consider these suggestions:

- **Write a story that takes place on the way to the International Space Station.**

- **Write a story about the scariest moment of your life.**

Title: _____

_____

_____

_____

_____

_____

_____

_____

_____

_____

SECTION SIX: WORD PREVIEW
Welcome to your ten new favorite words!

When you encounter a new word, take a moment to consider what it might mean.

1. Think about the word and circle what part of speech you think it is. *(Many words can act as more than one part of speech, depending on how they're used in the sentence, **so only choose one part of speech below.**)*

2. Come up with a brief definition of the word in the part of speech you've chosen. It doesn't have to be the *correct* definition—just do your best.

feasible
Part of Speech: noun verb adjective

Definition:_____

_____

significant
Part of Speech: noun verb adjective

Definition:_____

_____

capable
Part of Speech: noun verb adjective

Definition:_____

_____

surmise
Part of Speech: noun verb adjective

Definition:_____

_____

interrogate
Part of Speech: noun verb adjective

Definition:_____

_____

recur
Part of Speech: noun verb adjective

Definition:_____

_____

avid
Part of Speech: noun verb adjective

Definition:_____

_____

corroborate
Part of Speech: noun verb adjective

Definition:_____

_____

anonymous
Part of Speech: noun verb adjective

Definition:_____

_____

modify
Part of Speech: noun verb adjective

Definition:_____

_____

feasible

fea·si·ble • [fEE-zuh-buhl] • \ ˈfēzəb(ə)l \

- adjective

1. possible to do easily or conveniently;

2. likely : probable

Jethro swore that he could cook me three hamburgers per day for a week, but I didn't think that was **feasible**.

SYNONYMS

ANTONYMS

WRITING TIME!

Use *feasible* in an original sentence of your own creation.

BONUS FUN TIME!

Express *feasible* with a drawing, or
invent a dictionary-style definition of your own.

significant

sig·nif·i·cant   •   [sig-nIf-i-kuhnt]   •   \ sigˈnifikənt \

- adjective
1. *sufficiently great or important to be worthy of attention;*
2. *having a particular meaning : indicative of something*

The hailstorm caused **significant** damage to every car that wasn't in a garage.

SYNONYMS

ANTONYMS

WRITING TIME!
Use *significant* in an original sentence of your own creation.

BONUS FUN TIME!
Express *significant* with a drawing, or
invent a dictionary-style definition of your own.

capable

ca·pa·ble • [kAY-puh-buhl] • \ ˈkāpəb(ə)l \

- adjective

1. *having the ability, fitness, or quality necessary to do or achieve a specified thing*

I'll have to chase my runaway sister because Owen just isn't **capable** of running that fast.

Synonyms

Antonyms

Writing Time!
Use *capable* in an original sentence of your own creation.

Bonus Fun Time!
Express *capable* with a drawing, or
invent a dictionary-style definition of your own.

surmise

sur·mise • [suhr-mIEz] • \ sərˈmīz \

- **verb**

1. *to suppose that something is true without having evidence to confirm it*

Based on what little information I have, I can only **surmise** that the cupcake was eaten by one of my sister's friends.

SYNONYMS

ANTONYMS

WRITING TIME!
Use *surmise* in an original sentence of your own creation.

BONUS FUN TIME!
Express *surmise* with a drawing, or
invent a dictionary-style definition of your own.

interrogate

in·ter·ro·gate • [in-tAIR-uh-gayt] • \ inˈterəˌgāt \

- verb

1. *to ask questions of (someone, especially a suspect or a prisoner) closely, aggressively, or formally*

My boyfriend came over for dinner last night, and my parents both **interrogated** him about his summer plans.

SYNONYMS

ANTONYMS

WRITING TIME!
Use *interrogate* in an original sentence of your own creation.

BONUS FUN TIME!
Express *interrogate* with a drawing, or
invent a dictionary-style definition of your own.

recur

re·cur • [ri-kUHR] • \ rəˈkər \

- verb

1. to occur again periodically or repeatedly

This problem will certainly **recur** unless we figure out how to make it stop for good.

SYNONYMS

ANTONYMS

WRITING TIME!
Use *recur* in an original sentence of your own creation.

BONUS FUN TIME!
Express *recur* with a drawing, or
invent a dictionary-style definition of your own.

avid

av·id   •   [Av-uhd]   •   \ ˈavəd \

- adjective

1. having or showing a keen interest in or enthusiasm for something

Yenni is an **avid** rock climber, so she goes climbing every weekend.

SYNONYMS

ANTONYMS

WRITING TIME!

Use *avid* in an original sentence of your own creation.

BONUS FUN TIME!

Express *avid* with a drawing, or
invent a dictionary-style definition of your own.

corroborate

cor·rob·o·rate • [kuhr-rAHb-uhr-rayt] • \ kəˈräbəˌrāt \

- verb

1. to confirm or give support to (a statement, theory, or finding)

I would be more inclined to believe your story if you could find any solid evidence that would **corroborate** it.

SYNONYMS

ANTONYMS

WRITING TIME!
Use *corroborate* in an original sentence of your own creation.

BONUS FUN TIME!
Express *corroborate* with a drawing, or
invent a dictionary-style definition of your own.

anonymous

a·non·y·mous • [uh-nAHn-uh-muhs] • \ əˈnänəməs \

- adjective

1. (of a person) not identified by name : of unknown name

Sometimes a journalist will keep her sources **anonymous** in order to protect them.

SYNONYMS

ANTONYMS

WRITING TIME!
Use *anonymous* in an original sentence of your own creation.

BONUS FUN TIME!
Express *anonymous* with a drawing, or
invent a dictionary-style definition of your own.

modify

mod·i·fy   •   [mAHd-uh-fie]   •   \ ˈmädəˌfī \

- **verb**

> *1. to make partial or minor changes to (something), typically so as to improve it or to make it less extreme*

We **modified** our initial design for the skate park in order to make it more accessible to observers.

SYNONYMS

ANTONYMS

WRITING TIME!

Use *modify* in an original sentence of your own creation.

BONUS FUN TIME!

Express *modify* with a drawing, or
invent a dictionary-style definition of your own.

SECTION SIX: WORD REVIEW

Congratulations on learning ten amazing new words! Remember that the whole point of learning new vocabulary is actually to use it, so let's put your new vocabulary to use.

1. Review the words you've learned. Consider what ideas come to mind when you say the words. How about when you read the definitions?
2. Circle at least **two** of your favorites. You'll get to use these when you write your very own story!

feasible —— adjective
1. possible to do easily or conveniently;
2. likely : probable

significant —— adjective
1. sufficiently great or important to be worthy of attention;
2. having a particular meaning : indicative of something

capable —— adjective
1. having the ability, fitness, or quality necessary to do or achieve a specified thing

surmise —— verb
1. to suppose that something is true without having evidence to confirm it

interrogate —— verb
1. to ask questions of (someone, especially a suspect or a prisoner) closely, aggressively, or formally

recur —— verb
1. to occur again periodically or repeatedly

avid —— adjective
1. having or showing a keen interest in or enthusiasm for something

corroborate —— verb
1. to confirm or give support to (a statement, theory, or finding)

anonymous —— adjective
1. (of a person) not identified by name : of unknown name

modify —— verb
1. to make partial or minor changes to (something), typically so as to improve it or to make it less extreme

STORY SIX

1. List the words you've chosen:

_____

2. Write a story that incorporates all of your chosen words. If you can't think of anything to write about, consider these suggestions:
   - **Write a story inspired by the most annoying thing that a member of your family does.**
   - **Write a story that takes place in a carnival House of Mirrors.**

Title: _____

_____

_____

_____

_____

_____

_____

_____

_____

_____

Wonderful Words for Eighth Grade Vocabulary & Writing Workbook ©2021 Grammaropolis LLC

INDEX OF WORDS USED

Printed in the USA
CPSIA information can be obtained
at www.ICGtesting.com
JSHW060042150824
68134JS00028B/2603

9 781644 420584